# Dobie
The Canine Saint

Excerpts from reviews from the first edition of
**DOBIE THE CANINE SAINT**
*runner-up for the Indie Excellence Award*

The link between dog and owner is a strong one, with great spiritual benefits. A touching tale of the link between pet and master, *Dobie: The Canine Saint* is a must for dog lovers and community library pet and wildlife collections.

    Midwest Book Review

A well written, emotional, easy to read work that actually teaches you something and in the end leaves you feeling pretty good about things ... this little book is certainly going to leave you with a lot to think about; such things as your relationship with other humans, other creatures and most importantly, your relationship with yourself!

    Don Blankenship (Top 50 Reviewer)

This is a memoir from real life, and it is the tale of a man and his dog. It is exactly what it claims to be, a spiritual love story, easy to read and leaving the reader a little wiser but not really sadder.

    David Bryson (Top 1000 Reviewer)

I can appreciate the sentiment of those who find more than just a companion in animals: they can heal us and bring us into a fuller appreciation of all life has to offer. And that is the main message of this wonderful little book.

    Fritz R. Ward (Top 1000 Reviewer)

What an absolutely beautiful story about the love of a man for his dog AND the love of a dog for her person! As a dog-lover, this is truly a story that reached out and grabbed my heart.

  Kathy W. (Top 1000 Reviewer)

This is definitely a tear jerker, so grab your Kleenex, but I think the relationship between Dobie and Paul, and the amazing spiritual imprint Dobie left on his life, and the lives of others she met, is well worth the puffy eyes I am now suffering ... it's an extraordinary tribute to a man's best friend.

  Cherise Everhard

Bottom line: Paul Greenbaum's pleasant New Age style relates the journey of Dobie's life to the spiritual journey of his master like a modern-day 'Siddhartha.'

  Diana Faillace Von Behren

*Dobie, the Canine Saint* is profoundly moving. It has been years since I have been so touched by a book, but it is more than that; as the warm tears rolled down my cheeks, the eyes of my soul were opening to a clear reality, the certainty that love is the greatest truth, and it comes to us in many forms.

  Alejandra Vernon (Top 500 and Hall of Fame Reviewer)

The book has it all, humor, tears, frustration, sadness, and in the end death. But it is so worth the read. And yes the book reminded me that I do indeed like animals more than many humans.

  Beth DeRoos (Top 1000 and Hall of Fame Reviewer)

# DOBIE
## The Canine Saint

PAUL GREENBAUM

Healing from the Heart Publishing

Dobie, the Canine Saint

© 2007 Paul Greenbaum

All rights reserved. No part of this book may be used or reproduced in any manner whatsoever without written permission except in the case of brief quotations embodied in critical articles and reviews.

HEALING FROM THE HEART PUBLISHING

Edition ISBNs
Trade Paperback: 978-0-9796483-0-4
E-book: 978-0-9796483-1-1

Second Edition 2013

This edition was prepared for printing by
The Editorial Department
7650 E. Broadway, #308
Tucson, Arizona 85710
www.editorialdepartment.com

Cover design by Kelly Leslie
Book interior design by Morgana Gallaway

*Your light and your love have helped me to find my own.
Thank you, dear friend and companion.*

# The Meeting

Late August, the tail end of a hot, sticky New York summer. It felt like a hundred degrees in my car as I headed up I-95 north to meet my friend Tom for a camping trip in Maine. Tom was teaching biology to underprivileged children at a school tucked away in one of the most rural sections of Vermont. After seven hours on the road, I arrived at twilight. Usually this far north, a cool breeze washes over even the hottest of days like a welcome friend, yet this particular evening, the stifling humidity didn't abate.

I thought it odd that Tom walked over to my car the instant I pulled up and stood waiting as I hoisted myself out of the seat, my sweaty legs sticking to the vinyl. After hurried greetings, he said, "I've got to show you something."

"Hope it's the bathroom, 'cause I've got to pee something fierce."

Tom hurried me into the small house. After I used the john and gave his wife a quick hello, Tom marched me back outside.

Although a free spirit and at times prone to unexpected behavior, Tom had always been a good host, so I was surprised he hadn't let me get settled, but I was too tired to complain. Tom led the way to a dirty cage fashioned from scrap wood and chicken wire. The walls were low enough that with the top closed, the three skinny puppies inside couldn't quite stand upright.

"Look at them," Tom said.

No, not puppies. Big Pal, a companion of twelve years, had been put to sleep only a few days before this trip. Dogs, any dogs, scraped a terribly raw nerve. But I took a deep breath and glanced at the puppies.

"So?"

"Look!" he said. "I mean really look." Tom moved behind me as if to physically direct my focus.

The pups, about five months old, appeared to be mostly Doberman. They looked ordinary enough despite their terrible living conditions.

As I stared numbly at the puppies, I began to get a peculiar feeling. A faint buzzing started up in my mind, like a bothersome mosquito nose-diving at my consciousness. My intuition was warning me to pay attention, yet I was too busy pining for a shower or a cold beer—or better yet, both.

Tom's voice brought me back to the present. He held up his favorite from the litter. "Why don't you take this one? Her name's Vicious."

Take it where? I thought we were going camping.

I studied the pup, an emaciated female. She was obviously extremely timid, scared to the point of seeming emotionally disturbed. "Vicious, huh?"

"When I got here at the beginning of summer," Tom said,

"they couldn't have been more than eight weeks old. My next-door neighbor owns the mother, part Rottweiler. The dad's pure Doberman. He's trying to sell the puppies, but so far, no takers."

I nodded slightly.

"Their cage is practically right under my window." Tom glanced toward his neighbor's cottage and lowered his voice. "He doesn't take good care of them. They don't get enough to eat. And he lets the schoolkids torture them—yell at them, squeeze their paws, drop stones or firewood on them."

The children were probably reenacting a version of the way they'd been treated.

"Take Vicious home," he said. The owner'll bitch I just gave her to you, but he'll get over it if he knows she's getting a good home."

I looked at him noncommittally.

"You'll be saving her life," he said. "Look at her. She's a great dog."

I looked at Vicious for a long moment. No denying she was cute, but behind her bright puppy eyes were sadness and deep, palpable wounds. All about her was an aura of tenuous fragility and distrust in life.

But even if she'd been normal, I had no desire for a Doberman, as they tend to be high-strung and hyper-nervous. I like the earthy, happy-go-lucky personalities of hunting dogs. German shorthaired pointers, like Big Pal, were my favorite. Dobermans' angular bodies, cropped ears and tails looked artificial to me.

As if reading my mind, Tom said, "You'll have to crop her ears, but the owner did the tail when she was just a few days old. Know how it's done?"

"Do I want to?"

"They wrap the tail tightly with a rubber band, the blood's cut off, and the bone dies. After a while you can snap it right off with your fingers. Supposedly they don't feel a thing."

I nodded. "Sure. Just like a baby boy doesn't feel anything when they chop off his foreskin. Why wouldn't any young, tender being feel its own body being mutilated?"

"I don't remember being circumcised," Tom said. "Do you?"

I tapped my head. "It's in here somewhere." I glanced at her thin, slightly droopy ears. They gave her a friendlier look, but sick or healthy, cropped ears or not, I didn't want another dog so soon after my last one had been put to sleep.

Night was rapidly falling. Crickets and cicadas had begun a mad chorus, and hundreds of fireflies appeared in the fields, blinking magically in the humid air. A mosquito bit me on the arm and another on the back of my neck. "Forget it, Tom. Can we go inside now? I'm getting eaten alive." We ate a late dinner and slept. Early the next morning, we left for Maine.

As we crossed the border into New Hampshire, fingers of light were just breaking into an overcast, motionless sky. The roads were wet, and the temperature had dropped thirty degrees. We stopped in Rangeley, Maine, to pick up supplies and then piled back into the car and drove to Lake Aziscohos. We hiked out and set up camp on a bluff overlooking the remote lake. That night the temperature dropped lower, and heavy rain fell throughout the week.

I didn't mind being forced by weather to stay in the tent. I secretly enjoy being spared the obligation of doing anything strenuous, and except for preparing food and brief bursts of exercise, I curled up in my den, as would any sensible animal.

I lay on my sleeping pad and read, frequently dozing off to the rhythmic patter of the rain on the canvas, the daffy cries of the loons, and the soft lapping of the water on the sand.

The forced confinement of the tent and the almost-sacred stillness of the land loosened my thoughts. I glanced at Tom, already in his sleeping bag reading a book. I never thought we'd become such good friends, especially after the strange way we'd met ...

A year and a half ago, on a dark morning in Stowe, Vermont, we first crossed paths. I was skiing alone on the empty slopes, the fog so thick you could barely see beyond the tips of your skies. Just as I was about to catch the chairlift, a man appeared out of the heavy stillness and, in a spray of snow, materialized next to me.

"Mind if I ride up with you?" he asked.

"Not at all." Off we went.

We settled into our seats and, with the steady clank of the chain in our ears, were lifted over pines nearly hidden in the white, swirling vapors.

"You know, the ski business has degraded into a circus," Tom said, his eyes bitter. "The idea isn't to actually teach people to ski but to sell real estate. I think the ski instructors get a bonus every time they take the student past the condominiums."

I nodded my head, neither agreeing nor disagreeing.

"It's a dog show. With their Gucci ski suits and five-hundred-dollar fur hats, they can't ski a hill of beans. Vermont used to be about skiing. Not anymore."

Tom seemed a likable enough fellow. His loquaciousness was a perfect complement to my long periods of silence. He let out his breath with a cloud of steam. "I've been watching you.

You're a pretty good skier. But you could be a lot better—if you had the right teacher."

"I've had lessons before. I'm sure I'll take them again."

"Why not now?" Tom asked. "I'll only charge you fifty bucks for the rest of the afternoon. To get a teacher as good as me, that's a bargain. Fifty dollars a minute would be a more honest price for what I'm going to show you. Take lessons from the bozos who work here and you might end up with a condo, but I doubt you'll learn to ski. What do you say?"

Under my goggles I raised my eyebrows. As a born-and-bred New Yorker who'd seen his share of scams, conmen, and street people, my first reaction to Tom's attempt to hustle me into ski lessons was suspicion. But he seemed genuine, and fifty dollars wasn't so much to gamble.

"Sure," I said as we got off the chair. "I'll give it a try."

"Stay behind me and do exactly what I do. Ready?" Tom shot out like a ball from a cannon. For a second I stood gaping. I'd never seen a human being move so quickly on skis. In about five seconds he was so far ahead I could barely see him, much less follow. I'd fancied myself a decent skier, but in Tom's wake I felt clumsy. He led us to an icy hill so steep our skies stuck out over the top.

"Ice is a good teacher," he said. "Come on!"

His kamikaze style left no room for hesitation. I took a deep breath to control the anxiety in my gut and pushed off with my poles. On the first turn, I caught an edge, fell heavily, and slid down the entire hill on my stomach. When we reached the bottom I got to my feet and, before Tom saw me, scooped out the snow that had wormed under my clothes. Tom turned around with a big smile. "Wasn't that great?"

I tried to hide the frustration that comes after putting in forty days a season for ten years learning how to ski and then coming upon a master who made me look silly. "Just perfect."

By the final run of the afternoon, Tom had gained my respect, and a solid bond of friendship had been cemented. Since then he'd proved himself a deep thinker who challenged many of the normal tenets of the American dream. Tom made a living skiing and fly-fishing. I found it hard to imagine that his day at the office took place on a mountain or beside a softly moving river. I didn't know very many people who actually did what they loved.

The rain let up briefly and I went outside. The drenched earth was exhaling the fragrance of a ripening summer. Twilight was rapidly approaching, and everything was still. Little beads of rain hung on the firs, glistening like transparent jewels, and occasionally dropped into the water with a soft plop. A family of loons glided onto the mirror-like surface, and I spied a moose walking on an island in the middle of the lake. What a fine bit of country this is. The earth seemed to have a happy feel, as if the spirits of the land were at peace.

I've felt it before in large tracts of unspoiled wilderness. I took a few deep breaths, swung my arms back and forth, and entertained the idea of building a fire and making dinner—but it was freezing. I got back into my bag and shut my eyes. Just before sleep, my thoughts floated lazily. *I'm glad to be here with Tom, but I wish I were sharing this with a woman.* While the desire was real enough, the prospects were unlikely. I lived by myself and hadn't had a girlfriend for over a year.

A week later, we returned to Vermont, and I spent a last night at Tom's place. In the morning I packed up my gear. After more than seven days of heavy storms, the weather finally cleared. An almost-warm sun was trying to dry the rain-drenched earth, and a light breeze blew fluffy clouds, intensely white against the freshly washed sky. Everything was clean, with a strong hint of fall in the air. I loaded my stuff into the car.

"You sure you don't want to take Vicious?" Tom raised his eyebrows almost pleadingly.

Why was he pushing this dog so persistently? Mostly to humor Tom, I pretended to consider it one last time. I knew I didn't want the dog and opened my mouth to say so, but a quiet, sure voice inside me caused the words to die before they reached my lips. Take her. Take the dog.

Just because I trust my inner voice doesn't mean I always agree with it or follow its orders, and I sure questioned it this time. I don't want another dog and certainly not this one. Better to complete the grieving before getting another.

But the voice was firm. Take the dog.

Lost in mental inertia for a full thirty seconds, I said nothing as Tom looked at me intently. I was on an inner fence, teetering toward leaving the dog in its dirty cage and getting back into my car. Certainly that seemed to be the most prudent course of action.

I shook my head no, but to my utter surprise, my mouth said, "Okay." Tom's jaw dropped, but he didn't miss a beat. "Hold on, I'll get her." He ran over to the cage and returned with the dog in his arms.

I took the scared, skinny puppy by her collar and attempted to put her in the backseat of my car. Vicious snapped out of her passivity and struggled to get away. She planted her feet and dug her claws firmly into the mud. I picked her up tightly in my arms, but she wriggled so frantically I could barely get her past the door. Finally, with effort—and some scratches to my arms—I got her into the backseat and closed the door. She lay as stiffly as a nervous statue as we drove through the magnificent New England countryside.

After about an hour on the road, I heard Vicious moving around. Finally she was settling down. I looked in the rearview mirror to see her squatting on the backseat, urinating.

"No!"

She leaped in fear, and a stream of diarrhea sprayed over the seat and slopped onto the floor mats.

"Wonderful." I pulled to the side of the road and searched for something to clean up the mess. All I could find was an old newspaper, which did little more than push the poop around and shove it behind the backseat. "Even better."

I got a blanket from the trunk and laid it out so Vicious wouldn't have to sit in her own filth. Almost immediately, she lay down and fell asleep. As we drove back to my home in Putnam Valley, New York—with the windows open to counter the stink—I was already regretting my decision.

# Fear

Home was a magical place nestled between forest and a three-mile lake. Complacent, well-fed deer feasted on grasses less than twenty feet from the house. Raccoons and opossums were as abundant as squirrels, and huge hawks rode the currents high above the hills, searching for food. Occasionally I caught a fox off guard at dusk or in the early morning, and it would disappear like a ghost into the thick shadows of the hardwoods. At night a community of screech owls flew from tree to tree and called to each other until dawn, their mysterious voices never failing to evoke wonder.

Long ago, small family farms dotted the land, but they'd mostly been sold, and at the turn of the century, summer homes mushroomed around the lake. In recent years, people had started fixing up the dilapidated cabins. They added heat and insulation and, like me, lived here year-round. But transients still outweighed the permanent residents, and in the fall when the vacationers went back to the city, ancient trees shed deep layers of gold and scarlet on the abandoned properties. The gardens rejoiced in the absence of caretakers, and overgrown plants thrived in the fertile black soil.

After seven hours on the road, I pulled into the driveway and turned off the engine. I stayed behind the wheel for a moment to gather my wits. Vicious was clearly nervous as I lifted her out of the car, and after the backseat poop fiasco, I wanted her to be relaxed before going into the house. I carried her to the back yard and set her on the grass in the full afternoon sun. She didn't move but sat stiffly, seemingly wondering at this strange turn in her life.

Normally I'm not a talkative guy, but I said softly, "It's okay, Vicious. This is your home now, and you and I are going to be good friends." She didn't respond. After about half an hour, the peace of the land seemed to seep into her. She relaxed a little and her breath came more easily.

After I'd had Vicious home awhile, it was clear that life with her would be challenging. She barely let me touch her. If I made too quick a motion toward her, she'd quail and wet the floor. I learned to move slowly and speak softly. I put her food close by and left the room so she could eat alone. Mostly, she liked sitting on her bed, a round pad with a faded plaid cover, a hand-me-down from Big Pal, that lay in a corner, partially hidden by the massive wood stove. From her protected den, as I went about my chores, she watched me with fear and suspicion.

Why she rarely strayed far from her bed except to defecate on the nearby rug was at first a mystery. But I soon discovered that to Vicious, the large Oriental rug in the living room was the only safe harbor in a sea of slippery, noisy wooden floors and slate tiles. A touchy situation: if I grabbed her collar she'd pee. So I swung open the door and let the fresh air do the talking. Her nose twitched at the mysterious fall smells.

"Come on, girl," I said softly. She inched slowly off the rug, but as she got toward the middle of the wooden floor, she panicked, her back legs frantically slipping and skating until she made it to the safety of the doormat. The return trip was the same except in reverse. As she performed this scurrying dance, her nails made a desperate tap dance that could be heard anywhere in the house. Her floor phobia was easy solved with throw rugs and runners placed strategically around the house.

Other things weren't so simple.

On Halloween that first year, a knock at the door triggered snarling and barking like a crazed junkyard dog's. I looked through the peephole. Standing on my tiny porch and spilling down the stairs were a fairy princess, a couple of ghosts, a skeleton, a grim reaper, and four adult chaperones. When I opened the screen door, Vicious rushed at them. The parent in front gasped and shielded her child with arms and body. I barely grabbed Vicious in time. They all moved back a few steps, and how could I blame them? Even I didn't know if she was capable of sinking her teeth into the flesh of a little trick-or-treater.

"New dog?" one parent said in a quiet voice, looking surprised that I'd have a dog like her. I nodded and wondered again why I'd taken Vicious and to what degree she'd cramp my lifestyle. I left the candy in a large bowl outside with a sign that read, "Help yourself." But a closed door didn't stop Vicious from having a bloody fit if someone came near the house.

One of the reasons I love the country is that dogs can go free. But with Vicious I needed to be careful, even in the forest. We did our runs weekday nights or early mornings, and I picked isolated areas where, I hoped, we wouldn't see anyone. One morning, an older couple started down the trail, and before I could restrain her, Vicious raced toward them. When they saw her charging at full gallop, they both froze. The woman swooned and braced herself against a tree to keep from falling, her other hand clasped over her heart. Vicious had them cornered—teeth bared and barking—by the time I reached them. I quickly grabbed her by the collar and pulled her away from the terrified couple. The husband was furious. In a heavy German accent, he scolded me.

"My wife has a bad heart. Your dog could have killed her! If she had a heart attack, I would have you arrested and put in jail." He glared at me. "Your dog should be killed. An animal like that should not be allowed to live, much less roam freely."

"I'm terribly sorry. I'll keep her on the leash." As the couple went on their way, still sending me angry daggers with their eyes, I shook my head. I had no experience with emotionally damaged dogs. When I'd accepted her into my life, I'd figured a little tender loving care and enough to eat would heal just about anything, but now I considered that perhaps I'd signed myself up for a job I couldn't handle.

Deworming and two months of good food had put a layer of fat and muscle over Vicious' protruding ribcage, and her coat gleamed like a black mirror. But on the inside, something had been crushed and was still bleeding. Was it even possible for her to be healed? If so, how? Yet I sensed that behind her large, fearful eyes was a deep longing to connect.

I liked to watch her as she slept. In her dreams, there was no trace of tension or fear. Her face was peaceful, almost angelic. While watching one day, a strange, unfamiliar sentiment moved in my breast. It was that wordless contract a parent makes when he gazes upon his sleeping baby. My soul moved toward hers, I took her as mine. In the depths of me, I made a vow to care for her for the rest of her life. If only her heart could always be at peace, as it was now in her sleep. Yet I knew that the wounds of the heart and soul aren't healed at once, but as slowly as hair grays. And although I'm not a patient man, in the depths of my soul, I was willing to wait.

# The Early Years

The first time I laid eyes on Ginger, I was lying naked in a lounge chair, soaking up the last rays of a diminishing fall sun. Vicious was asleep on the ground next to me when a strange car pulled up to the vacant next-door cabin. As if on a spring, she neurotically shot up and trotted over, growling like a banshee. While I hastily put on my pants, a deeper growl and a high-pitched yelp of pain pierced the air. Vicious scurried back—her tail and entire rump curled under—with an older German shorthaired pointer in hot pursuit. The pointer looked so much like Big Pal that my eyes popped open and my heart flip-flopped. For a few seconds, I was disoriented. I'd seen him so many times in this very landscape. It can't be. I put him in the ground myself.

A man with a teenage girl and a woman carrying a newborn baby walked up. "I'm sorry Ginger nipped at your dog."

"I'm sure she deserved it."

A few days later, Ginger came to the front door. When I opened it, she waltzed in as if she owned the place. Vicious hadn't forgotten their initial meeting and disappeared, tail tucked, to the safety of her bed. After casing the establishment with her nose, the portly old hound scrounged Vicious' leftover dinner, curled up on the couch, and snored for the rest of the afternoon. The second time Ginger scratched at the front door, Vicious wagged her tail excitedly. Somehow the ice between them had been broken, and as the weather grew cooler, Ginger became a regular visitor.

Maybe it was because she looked so much like Big Pal, but I couldn't help falling in love with Ginger—dogs sense that. She was over so frequently that she became more my dog than the neighbors', who had their hands full with kids. They didn't seem to mind that she slept at our place and even went on vacations with us. Under Ginger's live-in tutelage, Vicious learned the facts of life. Whatever the old dog did, the puppy watched and copied. That's how she learned that the couch is a better place than the floor. But more than being a teacher, Ginger was a friend and the first to be let into the inner chamber of Vicious' heart.

One fall day, both dogs were out in the yard. Ginger advanced toward Vicious shuffling outrageously, with lowered head, making an unearthly noise, somewhere between a whine and a houndlike Bruce Lee "kiai"—a fighting yell. After looking dumbfounded for a long moment, a lightbulb flashed in Vicious' head. She clumsily rushed at Ginger. The older dog tucked her head, protected her neck, and circled away from the attack like a four-legged boxer. Vicious instinctively danced and circled, but experienced Ginger lunged and nipped the loose skin of Vicious' throat. She yelped loudly in pain, but it just fueled her desire to learn the game. She rebounded forcefully, a nonstop blur of activity. When Ginger had had enough, a low growl was all it took to signal "game over."

By winter, the gawky, angular Vicious was three inches taller at the shoulder, and her endurance far better than the elder dog's. On a cold, sunny morning, as they spun and circled together in six inches of snow, old Ginger's back legs buckled for an instant. Vicious seized the opening, and her razor-sharp puppy teeth, which had yet to be dulled by bones or worn down to nubs from carrying rocks, got in a good nip. Ginger's loud yelp of pain immediately switched into an authoritative bark. Vicious quickly submitted belly-up. Ginger walked off stiff-legged but proudly.

All seasons, I ran the dogs on a rutted dirt ribbon that coiled through a jungle of green hills. One day as I ran full speed, I spied the dogs wandering off. I veered from the path, hid behind a tree amid some dense underbrush, and waited. When they noticed I was gone, they ran down the road but couldn't find me and then panicked and galloped back and forth up and down the dirt track. I had to bite my tongue so as not to laugh out loud. Finally Ginger, the old hound, caught on to the game. She screeched to a halt and put her nose to the ground. Vicious, of course, followed suit. Their zigzag path soon had them staring at me, tongues lolling, as if to say, "What the hell are you doing in there?" My future hiding places had to be more creatively planned. Once in a while I fooled them, but if they remembered to use their noses, they always found me.

In the first real heat of spring, we went down the hill to the lake. To the fat, overheated pointer, the cool water was a pot of gold at the end of a rainbow; she immediately hurled herself in as if entering nirvana. Vicious stood watching in disbelief as Ginger swam effortlessly, daintily gliding through the water with webbed paws. Ginger looked like she belonged in water. As usual, Vicious followed Ginger's lead and jumped in after her. But when she felt the weightlessness, she retreated quickly, like a movie run in reverse. Cool water, Vicious learned, is wonderfully refreshing, but from then on, she never allowed herself to go in over her head. She tentatively lowered her body and lay in the shallows, feet touching bottom at all times.

At the lake, I kept a canoe and a small sailboat. While the dogs hunted frogs, I hopped into the canoe and paddled around. Ginger Immediately jumped into the water and swam after me. Vicious barked and howled from the bank. From Big Pal, I knew German shorthaired pointers could swim for miles, and having Vicious barking and unattended was not something I wanted to chance. I quickly paddled back, and once on the beach, Ginger rushed over. Someone had taught her to ride in a boat, and with crotchety determination, Ginger bulled herself into the canoe.

Just to mess with Vicious, I stroked around in a tight circle with Ginger sitting in the middle of the canoe, regal as a duchess. Messing with Vicious even more, I paddled to the shore again and called her to join us. To my utter surprise, she approached the craft, barking with nervousness and excitement. I lifted her in, and she sat tensely, bracing herself with her front legs. When I pushed off, she scrambled around a little but then settled down and watched the scenery. From then on, Vicious was okay in the canoe, even on long trips.

In the winter, a silent blanket of white transformed the land into a mystery and the road into an icy track. The dogs barely noticed that I often slipped and fell as we ran, sometimes sliding many yards down a steep grade. In some ways, winter was best of all, for when we woke to thirty-below temperatures and three feet of fresh snow, all human life was absent. Had we stayed inside by the fire, we would have missed the long rays of the sun reflecting pastel colors through ice crystals, the rocks being faintly tickled by slow-moving water under a foot of yellow ice, and the indignant birds that, on a day such as this, acted as if no human would dare invade their sanctuary.

At night the three of us sat on the rug, basking in the heat of the huge wood stove. Vicious watched Ginger put her head on my lap and beg for love. The terror in Vicious' eyes soon softened into a sad longing. For a long time she remained shy and tentative, but one evening, she came over and put her head on my lap, just the way Ginger had. As I stroked her, she pushed into my hand for more. Sighing with pleasure, she rolled over to expose her belly.

"Why, you're a friendly girl after all." I scratched her stomach and leaned close. "But you don't let anyone know it, do you?" She looked up at me and shyly licked my face. In her eyes was the tenderness of a first love. It seemed as if she were trying out an exquisite new world but was still unsure and surprised that she was wanted. As we sat together, something opened. Her heart moved toward mine. She knew I was the one who'd provide and care for her, and in return, she loved me above all others.

By now her ridiculous name had been discarded. I'd renamed her Dobie.

# A New Home

In the fall, we packed up our peaceful nest and moved to the West Coast so that I could attend chiropractic school. Dobie was a five-year-old, seventy-five-pound Doberman—only an expert could tell from her slightly stockier body and more rounded snout that she had any Rottweiler blood at all. With the thousands of details, it was only two days before leaving that I thought about transporting the ultra-sensitive Dobie. I bought a carrier large enough for a Saint Bernard and called on the vet for advice.

"Let her sleep in the cage for a month," he said. "She'll get used to it."

I grimaced. "We're leaving in forty-eight hours."

He handed me a bottle of sedatives. "Give her a couple of these and put her in the cage tonight. At least she'll have one night."

When I gave Dobie the drug, she became so stoned she could barely walk. Even then, just the sight of the cage made her nervous, and after I forced her in and shut the door, she moped as if she were incarcerated.

Another poorly planned decision was Ginger—or better said, poorly faced. Though Ginger lived almost exclusively with us, I kept putting off asking the neighbors' permission to take her with us. On the day we left, I walked Ginger to the neighbors' place, knocked on the door, and gave her back. As Dobie and I turned toward our home, Ginger habitually followed, obviously wondering why she wasn't going with us. Dobie also seemed to sense something was strange. Ginger's family put her in the house and shut the screen door. The old pointer scratched the door and cried. As I walked away, a tightening across my chest told me I was making a mistake—but I turned away from the voice inside.

Dobie waited in the car while I checked my bags and set up her cage. I was nervous about bringing her into the hubbub of New York's Kennedy Airport and expected the worst. Sure enough, with the noise and the throngs of people frantically rushing around, she froze and practically had to be dragged into the terminal. But the instant she spotted her cage, she made a beeline right into it. I just shrugged. We'd made it past the first hurdle, but there was still a five-and-a-half-hour plane ride to survive.

I fretted about her the entire trip even though I'd put a large sign on her cage: "PLEASE TAKE CARE OF MY DOG." When I picked her up at the baggage claim, her worried eyes clearly told me she'd gone through an ordeal. Her blanket was soaked with urine, and she'd defecated in the carrier. The last five years had calmed her down, but she was still an exquisitely thin-skinned animal. I, too, was feeling overwhelmed as I balanced Dobie's carrier on one luggage cart and my suitcases on another. On the way to the rental car, I bent over the cage.

"Don't worry, girl," I said over the din of the airport, "another hour and this will all be over."

There was a persistent drizzle as we drove from the Portland airport to our new home in Rhododendron, Oregon. It was dark and the road unfamiliar. I missed the exit off the highway and cursed softly. Dobie picked up on my frustration. I looked in the rearview mirror at her curled up in the backseat between my suitcases. She seemed upset. It was after midnight when we arrived at our new country cabin, a modified A-frame under a canopy of dripping firs. I fumbled with the lock and, after finally getting it, swung the door open wide. All our familiar possessions were en route in a moving van. Before entering, Dobie sniffed the unfamiliar air and eyed the empty space suspiciously. But she followed me in without hesitation. We had a simple dinner and went right to bed. I rolled out a blanket and slept next to her in a sleeping bag. It was a home as long as we were together.

After getting set up, we explored the pros and cons of our new home. It was a great plus that we lived on the edge of the wilderness and good that the entire house was carpeted. The new place, although not much larger than our old cabin in Putnam Valley, had an upstairs, and Dobie didn't want any part of the spiral staircase. I slept upstairs in the bedroom, and she slept alone in a corner underneath the stairs. Since I'd be spending a lot of time in school, I installed a dog door for her to use. She watched with interest as I crawled through the opening, which was large enough for a dog twice her size. She even followed me out—once—but after the plastic flap closed behind her with a loud clack that startled her, she refused to use it. I felt like an idiot for ruining a gorgeous solid-oak door with a stained-glass window.

On the surface, Dobie appeared to have the same old phobias. Yet I sensed a stronger trust in me; she knew that whatever came our way, I wouldn't let her down. Like the day we were exploring the forest and the only way to get across a fast-moving river was over a rickety bridge. Bridges had always terrified Dobie, and she routinely avoided them, preferring to wade through the water to get to the other side. But as Dobie stuck her front paws into the water, I yelled for her to come. Though they may have looked similar, the rivers here were a different breed from the streams back East. The water wasn't deep, but the current was fast and powerful. If she swam, she might very well be washed away. She tentatively followed me over the bridge though it swayed and shook in the wind. Even a year ago, it would've taken an hour of pleading and cajoling before she'd allow me to get close enough to grab and carry her across. It may not seem like much, but even the most basic and common acts, things most dogs do instinctually, were great accomplishments and milestones for Dobie.

Near our home was a dilapidated cabin with three inches of moss and plants growing on the roof. In the yard sat an ancient Citroen that clearly hadn't been moved in years; the tires were pancaked and the entire vehicle was covered with fir pitch and needles. I wondered if anyone lived there, until I met the man—sort of. He was on his bicycle, and Dobie and I passed him while walking. I smiled and said hello, but he stared off and continued on his way as if I didn't exist. And it didn't happen just once; we seemed to be on the same rhythm. When I left my home or returned from work, I nearly always passed him on the road. Not to play his game, I'd wave or say hello, but he never looked at me. I knew he lived in the ramshackle cabin; I saw him park his bike and go inside and sometimes leave in the morning. I don't believe he was home except to sleep. He couldn't have worked, at least not at a conventional job. He was off riding his bicycle every day, all day, through almost any weather. I figured him for some sort of recluse or misfit, but I wasn't going to lose sleep over it. He seemed harmless enough, and every neighborhood has a few weirdos.

The low hills of the East tugged at our souls like an old friend, and we missed Ginger. A few weeks after we settled into our new place, I phoned the man who was renting our home in Putnam Valley to ask about her.

"That old dog kept coming here every day for about two weeks," he said. "She sat on the porch for hours and put some good scratches on your front door. Finally, she gave up and went home."

"How's she doing?"

"Her back legs got real stiff all of a sudden. Her owners put her to sleep just a couple of days ago."

My throat closed as my guilty heart rose into it. My first reaction was anger, and then I felt sadness. I shook my head. I could almost see her sitting on our porch wondering why we didn't hear her calls or open the door. How confused that sweet old dog must have been when we left. Removed from our family, her spirit shut down. Sure, there were excuses. Ginger had become an elderly dog with bad legs and a weak bladder. I'd had no idea what our life here would be like. Could I have handled two dogs with school? But no matter how many excuses

I offered, they couldn't ease the sting of regret I still feel about leaving Ginger behind.

"I should have kept her," I said in a whisper to the air.

I went outside and sat on the deck, and Dobie followed me out and sat next to me. I could imagine Ginger curled up on the couch, her warm brown eyes shining.

"I'm sorry I let you down, old friend. I should have seen you through to the end. I hope you know you will always live in our hearts."

# A Hike to Remember

The northwestern part of the United States, known for its wet winters, has a brief stretch of clear weather around the end of March. The sunny days in the middle of the seemingly endless rainy season are like bright patches on an otherwise-gray canvas. Locals call these "sucker breaks." The sunny, warm days lull us into believing that fair spring weather is here to stay, but alas, the rains always return with a vengeance. It was on one of these misleading Oregon March days, in our first spring out West, that Dobie and I went into the mountains and almost didn't come back.

I was off from school, and it seemed like a fine day for a long hike in the forest. Since I didn't know the area, a little firsthand exploration would be the best way to learn. I parked the car in the state forest a mile from home and started waking. Misty golden rays of the midmorning sun streamed through the firs but hadn't cleared the hills that rose sharply from the dirt road on which we walked. The temperature was perhaps 65 or 70, and I wore only a pair of shorts and a light flannel shirt. After a couple of miles on the road, I spied an unused-looking trail that headed invitingly up the mountainside. A sign warned that the trail was closed, washed out last spring and still not repaired. How does a trail wash out? My curiosity aroused, I started up. Deep ruts and sinkholes from erosion made for tricky footing. Fallen trees, like vanquished giants, lay torn in massive destruction. Branches and fir needles were scattered on the earth like an offering to nature and a testimony to the power she's capable of when she's stirred. I tried to imagine how the spring rains melted the snowpack, and water cascaded down the hills like waterfalls. The mud softened, and rocks slid and tumbled down, striking the rain-loosened trees in a roar of splintering chaos. I whistled slowly. I was sure glad I hadn't been up here when all this happened.

Even without the obstacles we had to climb over, the trail had a remarkably steep grade, and in an hour or so, the exertion began to tell on my legs. Dobie, not used to the warm weather, her tongue hanging out so far it seemed to be only inches from the ground, shot me a look as if to say, "Are you crazy?"

The trail continued to rise, and two more hours brought us to deep snowfields. I sighed with pleasure. Quite the novelty for an easterner. There had to be over fifteen feet of snow, and it was nearly April! Although I wasn't prepared for such terrain, the high daytime temperatures of the past few days had melted the top few inches of snow, which then froze again at night, making a fairly sturdy crust that supported our weight. The going was slow, but I felt compelled to continue. No one would work this hard to get up here if it weren't worth it, and I was too stubborn to turn back now.

We weren't disappointed. We emerged from the dark forest onto a ridge bathed in sunlight. Majestic Mount Hood loomed just ahead, clothed in a thick mantle of snow. It appeared to be near enough that one might reach it with a tossed stone. We weren't on the same earth of machinery, pollution, and technology but in another dimension where the elemental rhythm of life was yet untouched, and the only laws were those of nature. The magnificent beauty instantly lifted our spirits; Dobie and I forgot entirely about our tired bodies, and since the trail went on, we kept climbing. It was windy on top, and chilly air perfumed by the resinous fir and the change of season blew hard from the east. As the sun dipped in the west, an unearthly copper light reflected off the mountain, and the snowfields sparkled with golden light. Human sound was absent. The air pulsed with the thick vibration of silence, broken only by the low hum of the wind and the snow dropping from the trees. I was so light and free, and a glance at Dobie told me she felt the same. We played joyfully together in the snow.

The sharp chill that set in as the sun went down jerked me back to reality. We were basking in the sunset on top of a snowy mountain, four hours from the car, without any food or protection. Where had my brain been? Obviously, my common sense had also taken a leave of absence. But there was no time to chide myself. Immediate action was needed.

There was about an hour of twilight before nightfall. Not knowing what else to do, I ran full speed through the snowfields, occasionally slipping, losing my footing, and sliding down the steep trail. I ran as if in a race, fully aware that I was running for my life. Dobie thought it a game and enthusiastically joined in the chase. Within forty-five minutes, night fell with an inky blackness that made it impossible to see the thin ribbon of the unused trail. My mad dash through the snowfields had gained some time, yet we were still at least two and a half hours from the car—if I could see where I was going and if I could travel at a normal pace. It was now probably about thirty degrees, but as the evening progressed, the temperature would drop into the teens or lower.

We paused for a minute to plan our course of action. Staying and trying to make camp was out of the question. We had no protection, matches, or supplies. I was dressed in shorts! I cursed out loud. Entering the wilderness without preparation wouldn't be a mistake I'd repeat—that is, if ever got the chance to. Things looked grim, yet I wasn't worried; rather, I felt strangely elated.

We continued on, but I'd never experienced such pitch-blackness. I sat for a few minutes to get my eyes used to the lack of light and even tried the trick of looking out of the corners of the eyes, which are better able to see in darkness. Nothing worked. I found myself more frequently off the trail than on.

At one point I veered off course and couldn't find my way back. I seemed to be getting deeper and deeper into the brush. It'd been ten minutes since I lost the trail, and as I groped in the darkness on my hands and knees, the seriousness of the situation struck home. If I couldn't find my way down, I'd surely die from exposure. It wasn't as simple as heading down any way we could. This wasn't a hill but a mountain, in a wilderness that spanned hundreds of miles. The slightest deviation in the wrong direction would be disastrous.

What would become of Dobie? Even if she didn't freeze to death, how would she find her way back?

A rustle in the brush brought me out of my reverie. It was Dobie. She approached, sniffed me, and turned and headed back the way she'd come. Afraid she'd get lost, I followed her and found myself back on the trail. I walked a bit farther but was soon back in the brush, completely uncertain which way to go. Again Dobie found me and took me back to the trail. Finally, I got the message: she could see the path or, more likely, smell our footsteps from when we'd gone up and knew the way better than I. From then on, she led. If she moved too fast for me, I called her back. I wished she had a longer tail for me to hold on to, which would have made the journey a lot easier.

At this pace, the two and a half hours turned to four, and it was two hungry and weary souls who plodded off the mountain onto the road we had started on twelve hours earlier. At last, back in familiar territory! As we walked the final couple of miles to the car, a thin crescent moon rose over the hills. The stars glistened in the clear, frosty air. Spring had vanished. It was winter again. I took a long, deep breath. Getting into the old yellow Subaru and cranking up the engine had never felt so good. Nor can I remember ever having a dinner as fine as the one we had when we got home.

## Emotional Watchdog

In my senior year of chiropractic college, I got married. Dobie liked my new wife, but the relationship with her elderly dog, a far less playful companion than Ginger, was standoffish. My wife and I lived together in the A-frame for about a year before her children, an eight-year-old boy and a twelve-year-old girl, came to live with us.

This was my wife's third marriage, and her children had different fathers. The previous four years, while we were in school, the kids lived with their respective dads in another state. At first they were happy to be with their mom and, for the most part, accepted me with open hearts. There was so much to catch up on, but just as many hurts underneath the joy of being reunited. As well, roots may reach deep—so deep that cutting them isn't possible. The arid beauty of the high desert still ran in their blood and called to their souls. Rainy Oregon seemed dismal, and our home was so remote that not even a store was within walking distance. They missed their dads terribly.

When, in a blur of motion and noise, the children had first arrived, Dobie was eight years old. She didn't bark or growl but retreated under the stairs and sat frozen like a statue. Maybe she remembered her puppyhood trauma, but unlike the kids in Vermont, my wife's children liked her and treated her kindly. She watched them from her bed, seemingly trying to figure them out, but the scales tipped one day when the girl tossed Dobie a scrap of her dinner. From then on, when the kids ate, she stationed herself nearby, like a four-legged vacuum cleaner, to catch the freebies and accidents. Not only did she get used to my wife's kids, but she ran and played with them and even sought their affection. The tough scars that had held her heart captive for so long softened and finally dissolved. Her magnificent love then extended to everyone, including children.

For her thirteenth birthday, I bought my stepdaughter a puppy, a feisty mix of a Labrador and a poodle. As the blond, longhaired puppy grew, he tried to engage Dobie in play. Dobie hadn't had another dog to spar with since Ginger, but she happily jumped into the fray and easily overpowered the puppy. Dobie stepped into the role Ginger had served for her and took delight in the age-old ritual of the older dog teaching the youngster the facts of life. As the pup matured, he became a savvier sparring partner, but Dobie always possessed superior skills and size. At last, Dobie realized she was a powerful animal and didn't have to be afraid of other dogs.

She was still wearing these confident new shoes when our carpenter's dog, a large male Rottweiler, showed up. The hundred-pound male rushed over to Dobie and started sniffing her. He was the same height as Dobie but seemed twice as thick. She retreated slightly. This was a foreign type of play, the energy very different from the way it used to be with Ginger. But she gave it a try, circling around and playing with him. He moved quickly and tried to sniff her genitals. Quivering with tension, Dobie abruptly changed her position. When he attempted to mount her from behind, her sharp, authoritative bark stopped him dead in his tracks. He tried again, but Dobie nipped at him. After a few more tries he sheepishly backed down. I had to smile. She'd actually cowed this much larger animal. Even after that, though, I knew her self-confidence was, in part, an act. If she were ever to encounter a truly aggressive dog, I was certain, she'd turn tail and run.

Summers we camped in the wilderness, all of us, even the dogs, in one tent. Both children wanted me to be next to them, so I lay between, and again, the parent's heart moved in my breast. I stayed up long into the night feeling them against me, their soft breathing and midsleep movements the only break in the silence. The dogs lay at our feet in a tangle of bodies. Within the pack of our family, Dobie was comfortable and happier than she'd ever been—she blossomed. The different souls and personalities seemed to catalyze her growth.

Late one night, after my wife had already gone upstairs to bed and I was downstairs tidying up in the kitchen, I looked up and saw something that made me forget all about the pan I was scrubbing. Dobie—hesitantly, step by step—was creeping up the spiral staircase. Once she got to the top, I seized the moment, took her sleeping pad out from under the stairs, and put it at the foot of our bed. From then on, she used the stairs and slept in our room.

Another day soon afterward, a UPS truck pulled up to the house. It wasn't surprising that Dobie started barking, but when she put her nose to the dog door and shot out, I stood gaping. She'd never liked the way the plastic flapped, and she still bounded quickly away when she heard the noise, but it no longer stopped her from using it. It took five years, but the solid-oak door hadn't been ruined in vain.

Piling into the cramped cab of the yellow Subaru pickup and going for ice cream was a family ritual we all looked forward to. The dogs stayed in the flatbed. When we passed anyone walking on the road, the young poodle-Lab barked so uproariously that we all laughed. Dobie hung out, without our restraint, acting like the sanest member of the pack.

The drastic change from solitude to family life was harder for me than for Dobie. Except for a dog, I'd never lived with anyone for very long. But now, crammed into our thousand-square-foot, one-bathroom cabin were four humans, three dogs, a cat, and a pet rat. It was a living stew, and each of us contributed our own unique ingredients to the mix. It swirled and bubbled, but unlike with a recipe, the final result couldn't be predicted.

My wife and I loved each other, but we just couldn't make it work. The girl and her mom were like gasoline and a blowtorch, and the boy just wanted to go back with his dad. Currents of conflict seethed within our walls like riptides and undertows in the sea, and the weather could change in an instant.

My wife brought home a videotape course on child-rearing and implored me to watch it with her. There were a dozen tapes, and it took us over a month to get through them all. It was important, so the series said, for parents to be of one heart and mind, to maintain a unified front in raising children. My wife thought I treated her kids well, but she wanted me to participate more in the discipline, something I'd previously eschewed. My stepchildren already had fathers who loved them. If ever I overstepped my boundaries, they'd shoot right back at me, "You're not my dad. Who are you to tell me anything?" Being a stepdad is a delicate, potentially beautiful relationship, but I needed to know my place: friend, guardian, role model, perhaps, but not a father.

On a dark, rainy Saturday morning, I walked into a house thick with tension. The boy, now ten, was in a heated conversation with his mom.

"Did you take the money?" she asked.

"No!"

His mom grabbed my arm and the three of us held an impromptu arraignment in the bathroom. The boy sat on the toilet seat, his face desperate like a cornered animal's. His mom stood over him, interrogating like a lawyer. I felt sorry for the boy, but it was between them. I leaned against the wall and silently endured.

"There was money on that table, and now it's gone. Did you take it?"

"No!"

"Do you know who did?"

"No!"

Finally, after a prolonged grilling, he admitted to pilfering the cash to buy sweets. It was less than five dollars, but Mom stood on principle. "We can't allow him to steal." He was found guilty, and lying was added to the offense. Mom, now acting as judge, decreed that physical discipline was necessary.

Acting as a spectator to the kangaroo court was tiresome. But my place in all this became clear when my wife insisted that, as the man of the house, I execute the sentence. My palms got sweaty and my distaste turned into a knot in my guts.

As the three of us went into the living room, I caught my wife's eye. She nodded curtly, expecting me to take matters in hand. This is a man's job? I'd never hit a child. I didn't know exactly what to do. Would the boy simply drop his drawers like a sacrificial lamb and allow himself to be whacked?

He didn't appear to be in any sort of a submitting mood; he tore himself away from us in an attempt to abscond. A sharp glance from my wife told me to go after him. We were the adults, or so the videos on child-rearing had said—we couldn't let him walk all over us. Together, we had to show him who was boss.

I grabbed the kid, who was nearly as tall as I, and forced him to the rug. My inner voice was screaming to stop, but I didn't heed it, though every molecule of my being recoiled. My wife pulled down his pants, exposing his backside. I hit him halfheartedly with my open palm. The boy laughed. My wife looked at me. "He thinks this is a joke. Do it harder." I hit him hard enough that he yelled. I don't know if it was the pain of the spanking or because we, who were supposed to love and care for him, were perpetrating violence. Inside I was shaking, disgusted with myself. I vowed never to knuckle under to another's expectations and never to hit a child again.

As I went upstairs to get away from it all, I passed Dobie sitting in her corner. She was shaking with fear, seemingly in a state of shock. As an antenna picks up radio waves, she internalized the vibration in the air. And so I discovered Dobie had a profound ability. I affectionately called her "the great watchdog." Not a watchdog to protect the house from intruders—that would never be her lot in life. She was an emotional watchdog, and when she took her post, it was to harmonize the currents of negative energy that consumed our home.

After the spanking incident, the slightest rise of a voice in anger would cause Dobie to quake with fear. Even somebody muttering, "Oh, shoot," in an annoyed way made her uneasy. Not only could she perceive negative energy, but she also had an uncanny way of defusing it. Her quivering body, pleading brown eyes, and lowered head spoke to our hearts. She seemed to be saying, "Haven't you learned? Don't you see this is harmful?" Any argument would lose steam in the process of having to stop and pet her, until she finally responded with a softening of her worried eyes and a tentative wag of her tail.

In watching how she held her post, I discovered that a family has a soul. Unseen ties, like wires of great strength, bind us together. If one member of the family was content, all our lives improved. When one was injured, we all suffered. Each of us had a special place, and how we handled it affected everyone—like one domino striking another. If I had managed my place with the same temperament as Dobie did hers, my wife would have been happier, and her joy would have passed to the children. Although willing, apparently I wasn't ready or able to keep my center. The ties that connected us pulled, stretched, and groaned under the strain. Even with Dobie trying her best to neutralize our squabbles, the bonds sheared and snapped. We decided to separate and divorced soon afterward.

Once again, Dobie and I found ourselves alone. For a while after they left, it was difficult to be in the house. The quiet and solitude, once so comforting, now seemed terribly empty, and the memories of their laughter clung like ghosts to every room of the tiny place.

Yet we had grown through our brief four-year marriage. There were tender love-filled moments, times when the latent possibilities of life were palpably near. When the kids looked at me a certain way, I knew they needed me, and even if just in small ways, I was there for them. We rejoiced in the happy times, and in each other. After the family split up, I understood why Dobie had so thrived. Perhaps there was an element inside my loner heart not quite ready to handle a family, yet in the depths of me, I knew it was what life was all about.

# The Angel of Death

Early September. A strong wind jerked tired yellow leaves from the trees and scattered them on the car and the deck. The quick change of season seemed to reflect the breakup of our family. Dobie was eleven years old. Her legs were a little slower than they'd once been, and she spent more time resting by the fire, but her powerful body and shining eyes—still full of spirit and vitality—concealed the fact that she was an old lady for a Doberman.

The blow came suddenly and without warning. About ten o'clock, just before bed one evening, I walked up the stairs, expecting Dobie to follow. After fifteen minutes I called, and when she didn't come, I went downstairs to check. Dobie was lying on the rug, semi-paralyzed. She couldn't get to her feet, and her body shook with a slight tremor. Something seemed to be affecting her central nervous system, maybe a stroke or a tumor. I'd seen it before with dogs and knew that paralysis can come on awfully quickly.

Dobie sat like an injured bird that lacks the strength to fly and waits helplessly for death. Her eyes were dull, she looked old and worn out. Only a ghost of her spirit remained. I'd never had anyone this close to me die. How frail we are—one germ, one accident, an emotional shock and it's over. It had been a mere flicker of time since she was a puppy. Was it already time for her to go? How thin the line between life and death.

It was way too late to take her to our vet, but I'd heard of a twenty-four-hour emergency animal clinic in Portland. I called to make sure they were open, but when I tried to pick her up and get her into the car for the long drive, she growled and bared her teeth at me for the first and only time in her life. Not knowing what else to do, I gently massaged her and applied qigong (a Chinese medical technique), but neither seemed to help. Groping for anything that might ease her condition, I performed acupuncture, but she looked so miserable I took the needles out after a few minutes. She wanted only to be left alone.

After several hours, she allowed me to carry her upstairs and place her on her bed, beside my own. Feeling completely helpless, I pleaded with whatever gods were listening to look after my friend, regardless of what was to be. I turned out the light, but sleep wouldn't come.

In the early morning, I had a dream. I was driving my car, and Dobie was sitting in the backseat. Suddenly a stranger, a woman, appeared in the backseat right next to Dobie. She'd come for her—I knew it immediately—and, just as quickly, I determined that I wouldn't allow it to happen. The dream shifted. We were no longer in the vehicle but on open ground, facing off like gladiators about to engage in combat. I have had to fight before, but in each instance, I've felt reluctance. But why should combat bother me? I've fought in full-contact martial-arts competitions and spent many long hours in the boxing ring. Competition, however, is different from real fighting. Even the most brutal matches are mere sport. Your opponent may be trying to beat you into submission, but there's no real malice. It is more a test of one's skill, like a game of chess. Even after years in martial arts, raw aggression still frightens me.

This time I rushed in without hesitation. As we locked arms like wrestlers maneuvering to get the other off balance, I was astonished to feel the strength and determination of this woman. Never before had I experienced an opponent who came close to her overwhelming power. It was beyond anything human. Though seemingly an impossible feat, I managed to throw her to the ground and lock her arms in a way that put pressure on the elbow joint. I jammed the blade of my foot against her throat and turned my hip to exert hard pressure. Though I could barely contain her, I didn't dare let up. Dobie's life was at stake. After a bitter struggle, the woman gave in and I let her go. She simply smiled, shrugged, and walked away. I stood there for a long moment watching her stride off into the distance.

When I woke, I lay there with my eyes closed, trying not to lose the feeling. Strange dream! But was it a dream? I hadn't exactly been sleeping but wasn't completely awake either. Yet I was conscious the entire time. This was no dream. It was as real as anything that had ever happened to me—somehow even more real. Something extraordinarily profound had occurred, but what? Where had I been, and who was the woman I'd fought? It came to me with a shiver: the Angel of Death had come for Dobie last night, and I'd wrestled with her! My eyes quickly went to Dobie's bed, where I'd placed her the night before. From her bright eyes and comfortable demeanor, it was evident that her spirit was back in her body. She got to her feet, went downstairs easily, and exited through the dog door. I watched from the upstairs window. She sniffed around, walked normally, and ate a hearty breakfast. The signs of illness, which had been so serious only hours before, had vanished. What was I to make of this apparent miracle?

## Love Is the Miracle

Though Dobie looked fine, I immediately took her to Mark Evans, our vet.

"She had a real rough night." I explained her symptoms but not the dream.

He examined her for several minutes. "She seems okay. But let's take some blood and check out a few things." The results revealed nothing out of the ordinary.

That evening I was lying in bed with eyes closed. Sleep was as elusive as answers to the conflicting thoughts and questions that swirled through my mind.

Okay, so what happened last night?

Dobie, sitting beside me, jerked her head and looked at me curiously. But what did happen? How was Dobie miraculously cured, and what did my dream have to do with it? It seemed preposterous to think I'd literally fought the Angel of Death for my dog's life.

I made an appointment with Jen Clark, a therapist I saw occasionally. She wasn't the typical talk therapist—she was pretty far out—but I liked her because she had a way of cutting straight to the bone of my issues. She often pushed me past my comfort zone and artfully forced me to reveal parts of myself normally kept private.

She took one look at my face and whistled. "What happened to you?"

"I'm not sure."

"Tell me about it."

It was surprising how choked up I got while recounting the dream. Jen pretended not to notice.

"Dreams are real," she said, "oftentimes more real than our waking lives."

"Why's that?"

"While we're awake, the conscious mind filters what's too uncomfortable to face. In the dream state, the filter's gone. The hidden, unresolved stuff in the subconscious plays out."

"But in this dream I was awake, just like sitting here with you."

She nodded. "Dreams may be direct journeys into non-ordinary reality. Some have prophetic dreams, or even dreams of this nature."

"What nature?"

She smiled. "I've never had one like yours, you lucky dog. It's shamanic. Do you study shamanism?"

"I don't even know what you're talking about."

"The nature of the shamanic dream is … it is real. Maybe your perception was correct. Death had come for her. And … you also came … to fight for her life."

"But how?"

"Your soul—your pure essence—traveled to intervene for

her. Sometimes the dream state is the only possible place to deal with something like this."

I sighed. "I still don't know how such a miracle occurred."

"It is a miracle. The miracle of love."

"Love?"

Jen's eyes were a little sparkly. "Maybe you're no shaman, but your love made a bridge that reached beyond the physical. It was so strong, even the laws of nature were bent."

"How could a person's—or an animal's—time to die be bent?"

She laughed. "I don't think anything's engraved in stone. There's always the creative element that can change black and white into shades of gray if the situation calls for it. She must have had her part in it."

"What do you mean?"

"The will to live can never be underestimated. Take a man in a horrible accident who comes back after being in a coma for a month. Another woman, married for sixty years, dies from a head cold a few days after her husband dies. Perhaps one's given a choice whether to return or not. But those who do come back, despite the work and pain it might take, must really want to be here—or else there's a very good reason. Why do you think she did it?"

I could only guess. After my family split up, there was no one else to put my arms around, no one else to share love with. "Maybe she wanted to look after me."

"Maybe you're right. After seeing you fight for her life, she realized the extent of your love for her and the importance of your bond."

She must have seen the skeptical look on my face.

"Kahlil Gibran once wrote a story about a man and woman who truly loved," she said. "The woman got sick, and they were separated by death. But their love was so strong, they wanted to be together so much, they met in another lifetime. Their souls drew each other in like a magnet, and they recognized one another, even though they had different bodies. Is it any stranger with you and Dobie?"

I sighed. "I generally take that kind of stuff with a grain of salt."

Jen laughed. "It was your dream!"

Our conversation dried up for a long moment. Then Jen said, "Keep your eyes open. You may see some interesting things with that dog of yours."

I took that with a grain of salt also, but back at home, Dobie's eyes did seem to sparkle with a strange intensity.

# Re-creating a Purpose

Dobie's life did change. One morning she decided to accompany me to work, or better put, she refused to stay home. Ordinarily, as I left for work, she'd be hanging out in the house, sleeping on the couch. But on this day, as I started to drive away, the plastic flap slapped loudly. I looked in the rearview mirror to see Dobie shoot out of the dog door as if the house were on fire. She galloped after me a third of a mile down the driveway. It was more than merely strange—she'd never acted like this. For the previous twelve years, she'd been content to remain at home. I put her back in the house, but she stubbornly did the same thing again and again. I hoped an old dog like her would get tired, but she didn't, and being late for work, I finally stopped the car and Dobie jumped into the backseat.

After an hour's ride, we parked and walked down the busy, noisy street toward my office. I glanced at Dobie, trying to discern her mood. She'd lived her entire life in the country. Wouldn't the noise and bustle of the city frighten her? And how would she react to my patients' just strolling in without knocking? The last thing I needed in my chiropractic/acupuncture practice was a growling or barking dog. The landlord wouldn't appreciate it either. But she walked up the steps to my office without trepidation, and everything went better than expected. From that moment on, we were together twenty-four hours a day.

It was easy to see that Dobie came along not only to keep me company but also to help. She greeted each person as he or she arrived but served as so much more than a receptionist. My sessions lasted at least an hour, and I never knew exactly what course a treatment would take. While the patient was on the table, Dobie lay on the rug between the radiator and the person's head. As if her body were an irresistible magnet and the patients' hands made of iron, people dangled their arms over the table and invariably connected. Dobie seemed to sense the exact moment an individual was most in need. Especially while describing a stressful or emotionally painful incident, their hands instinctively reached for her. She became an important part of my practice.

During the yoga classes I taught, she'd spend a little time with each student. "That dog's a hambone," one man said. "She just wants attention." That wasn't quite the case. Nor was it completely accurate to say Dobie spread healing energy. It was more as if she neutralized nervous, unwanted energy. While watching her, I wondered if the canine species—pets in general—function as harmonizers. People think everyone loves pets because they provide unconditional love. Sure, everyone wants love, but even more important is the absolute need to give it, and sometimes the best way to give is to receive. But because so few are able to really receive, pets harmonize the cycle. Dobie provided a vessel into which people could put their love. I watched carefully and can testify to how she touched the heart of each person, for I could see the softness in their faces and the change in their eyes. They say old dogs can't learn new tricks, but Dobie had created a new purpose for herself.

# Goodwill Ambassador

In the two years following the Angel of Death's visit, Dobie's health seesawed wildly. Sometimes it was excellent, but other times, for no apparent reason, mysterious problems arose. Once, she stopped eating and drinking, ended up severely dehydrated, and spent two days in the hospital hooked up to an IV bag. The shadow of death came between us again, and it was weeks before she fully recovered her health. For several months, Dobie suffered intense pain. She needed help up and down the stairs and had to be lifted into the car. She'd lie on the floor and make noises somewhere between a cry and moan.

Chasing chipmunks had always delighted Dobie. The mere sight or sound of one would send her racing up the side of a mountain or keep her busy for hours digging up the earth where the little creature had vanished into its nest. She loved the game so much that I used to tell her that when we heard the chirp of a chipmunk, the little rodent was playing her song. But one crisp day while walking in the forest, we heard the distinctive call and spotted the quick flick of a wispy brown tail.

She instinctively charged but immediately cried out. Her eyes mirrored confusion. She'd chased chipmunks her entire life. It'd been a source of great pleasure. Dobie's head jerked around to look for a bee or some tangible cause of pain. Seeing nothing frightened her. She started to shake and turned back toward the car. In the weeks that followed, she didn't want to walk much or even get in the car.

Mark gave her a thorough examination. "Her vital signs and blood work are okay. Sure, she has a little arthritis, but not enough to be causing this much pain. In some ways, she looks better than she did a couple of months ago. What are you feeding her?"

"Just organic raw meat."

"Is that a change?"

"She used to get cooked turkey and rice, but I heard raw meat was healthier."

"From cooked food to all raw meat is quite a change. She likes it?"

"She eats it all."

Mark nodded. "Supplements?"

"A multivitamin/mineral, co-enzyme Q10, and fish oil."

Mark cast his eyes over her again. "I wonder if she could be going through a healing crisis."

"You think?"

He rubbed his chin. "It's a shot in the dark, but possible. With the totally pure enzyme-rich diet, she might be clearing out some old toxins. Maybe that's what's causing the mystery inflammation."

I'll never know exactly what it was, because, after a while, the pain disappeared, seemingly without a trace.

It was a time of change in many ways. Within the space of a month, I sold our country cabin, bought acreage not far from our former home, and purchased an office building in the city. I had only a few short weeks to pack, clean, and be out of both places.

Our last day there, Dobie and I were at the cabin, me sweeping up a pile of debris, Dobie sitting with worried eyes. Around us, in boxes stacked against the walls, were all our possessions. A knock came at the door.

It was the last person I expected: my neighbor—the man I'd seen nearly every day for the past ten years but who had never said a word to me—was standing on my porch.

I swung the door open and looked at him. He was trembling, his forehead bathed in sweat. I extended my hand as if seeing him here were an everyday occurrence. "Hello."

He raised his arm like the tin man in The Wizard of Oz, jerkily, as if it were stiff and rusty, and took my hand. His skin was clammy. I looked at him and waited.

"I see you're packing up."

I nodded.

"Well ... I just wanted to say I'm glad you lived here."

Ten years later! Somebody pinch me, I'm dreaming.

He seemed to be reading my mind. "I know, it's taken a while. But I have no use for most people. Most of 'em are clowns who show no respect or awareness, which is why I don't bother much with people anymore. But I watch everything. Like the way you take care of your dog. Most folks leave their dogs at home all day even if they're sick."

Dobie came over and nudged the man's hand. He looked at her eyes and stroked her head gently. A bead of perspiration dripped down his nose and fell onto his shirt. "How is she?"

"Getting old."

He nodded and paused uncomfortably, almost squirming in his own skin. "This isn't easy for me." He attempted a smile and, this time, extended his hand to me. "You were a good neighbor. I liked having you here." He gave me a card with a picture of a Buddha on it. On the back were his name and phone number. "If you ever need anything, give me a call."

I put the card in a safe place and, before resuming the cleanup, sat on the floor for a few minutes with Dobie. I'd thought the man was a misfit, but he was more aware and sensitive than most people. Dobie had somehow bridged the gap between us.

Soon we had a new home, if that's what you could call sometimes living at the office and sometimes in a yurt, a type of circular tentlike structure originally used by the nomads of Mongolia, which I'd erected on the open land I'd bought. The walls and ceiling were framed with two-by-fours, it had a plywood floor and even a skylight, but it was covered only with thin canvas. My office, unlike the yurt, had heat and running water, but neither place offered much comfort, not even a bed beyond a futon on the floor. But Dobie took it all in stride.

Now that we were part-time city folk, leashes, poop bags, and walks in the park were a necessity. After a long walk on a humid late-summer evening, we went over to a flat grassy spot where I liked to do yoga. I tried to perform a few postures while holding Dobie on the leash, but clearly that wasn't working, so I tied her to a small tree.

Ten minutes later a young Latina woman came over. "Is that your dog over there?"

I jumped up. I'd been so engrossed in my yoga that I hadn't noticed that Dobie had untied herself from the tree and strayed several hundred yards. She was standing at the base of the steep stairs, a high-traffic area where people were continually going up and down. "Sorry, I'll get her."

"She's not bothering anyone. It's just amazing the way she just stands there and smiles at people."

"Smiles?"

"You can always tell when a dog is happy. It smiles just like a person."

I looked at this woman more deeply.

"She's a beautiful dog," she said, "so very friendly. Guess I wanted to see what kind of person owns her."

"You've just met her, of course, but she's changed a lot."

"How?"

"She used to be a timid, fear-filled animal. Now ... I don't know how else to describe her: she's a goodwill ambassador."

The woman laughed. "Good description." She extended her hand. "Maria. I think I've seen you here before. Do you live nearby?"

"Just a block away."

"I'm in the neighborhood, too. Maybe we'll see each other again."

"I hope so," I said.

Dobie and I started taking walks in the park even more regularly.

## Learning the Secret of Love

I made an appointment with Jen Clark to talk about Maria, who had rather quickly become my new girlfriend. As I opened the door to her downtown office, her receptionist glared at us. "You can't bring your dog in here."

Jen popped in. "It's okay. The wonder dog can come in." She led us to her office, and once we'd settled in, she gave me a big smile. "Tell me about Maria."

"We get along well. She's intelligent, gorgeous. I like her a lot."

"Then what do you want to talk about?"

"There's one big catch."

"Oh?"

"She can't commit."

"Hmm. Don't be in such a hurry. In the beginning, it's better just to have fun. Committing comes later."

"She won't even commit to spending time together."

"What do you mean?"

"We're together nearly every night, but I'm never entirely sure she's coming. She never wants to be pinned down. So every night I wait, and at some time in the evening I might hear a knock on my door. If it's early, maybe we'll have dinner and catch a movie, if it's late—sometimes it's after midnight— we just make love and go to sleep. She stays till morning, and while I'm at work, she leaves."

"That must be crazy-making."

"Nervous-making, anyway. When it starts to get late, I leave the door unlocked and lie in bed listening for it to open. I'm not sleeping well."

"She doesn't call?"

"Sometimes. And she says she loves me!"

"Why do you think you've attracted a woman like that?"

"Attracted?"

"Why did life pair you with her?"

"What do you mean pair?"

"If you want to see what issues a person is dealing with, simply look at what life gives them."

"I still don't quite get what you mean."

"Life doesn't make mistakes. There's a reason for everything that happens."

I felt blood rush to my face and neck. "So if a woman's raped, you're going to tell me she needed it?"

"It's difficult to tell a woman who's been raped, or someone who loses their child, that it's necessary. But if a person wants to work with me, they've got to get out of victim mode and take responsibility for what's going on in their lives."

"How do you take responsibility for something that's not your fault?"

"Just like I said: there are no accidents in life. Whatever happens, we've somehow attracted it."

"Why would anyone attract a rape?"

"Life's showing them something for a reason. And that reason, ultimately, is to heal." Jen glanced at Dobie, asleep on the rug. "So how's your old dog?"

"Remember when you said there might be some interesting changes with her?" I described what had happened with my old neighbor.

"Interesting. Why do you think you kept crossing paths with that guy?"

I looked at her funny. "Why? We just did, that's all."

Jen raised her eyebrows and groaned. Just then Dobie cried in her sleep as if she were having a bad dream. I slipped down to the floor and placed my hand on her chest to wake her.

"It's a lot of work caring for a sick dog. How's it going?"

I paused, the gears in my head turning. How could I explain that when she felt pain, so did I; when she didn't eat, I enjoyed my food less; and when she tossed and turned at night, I couldn't rest? Anyone who's cared for an aging person understands the countless duties that must be performed to make him or her comfortable, and caring for an aging dog is no different. Each meal was made from scratch with the finest organic ingredients. Because she was old and shorthaired, she needed to be covered in cold weather, but each time she turned, her blanket slid off. I'd wake up many times a night to make sure she was covered and warm.

Words couldn't describe how I rejoiced with each sign of life in Dobie's body. When she ran, my spirit soared; when she had a good appetite, I was filled with happiness; I felt relief each time she had a decent bowel movement; when she smiled, I smiled; and when her eyes shone with joy, the joy in my own heart spilled over.

"The simple fact that she walks, eats, and shits makes me happy. The instant I wake up, I look down at her bed. When I see that she's still here, I'm grateful. Every day is a gift, because who knows when it's time for her to go?"

Jen looked at me in a way I hadn't seen before. Her serious expression held only a trace of a smile, but her eyes were soft and deep. There was so much feeling in her eyes that I was momentarily taken aback. She got up, hugged me, and kissed me on the cheek. I was surprised and embarrassed at this uncharacteristic display of emotions.

"Congratulations," she softly said.

"What for?"

"You ... you've become a mother."

I looked at her and waited.

"It's the highest kind of love. If a wife cooks, cleans, and performs sex, then the husband 'loves' her. But what happens if she doesn't feel like doing chores? What if she's ill and doesn't look good or feel like making love? More often than not, the man will leave. That's not love, it's a conditional exchange that says I'll do something for you if you provide me with something in return—a business deal."

Jen took a deep breath and let it out in a long sigh.

"The love you have for Dobie is the love of a mother. Your heart rejoices with her happiness. You suffer during each trial and tribulation. When she's sick, you nurse her back to health. You willingly sacrifice so she might be happy and comfortable. In other words, you've learned to love someone more than yourself."

Jen raised her voice a few notches. "This is the kind of love that will endure throughout time—like that story of Gibran's. When two hearts beat together, there's mutual sacrifice to please the other, but only good comes from it. There's no resentment over not getting what you may have wanted, because what you want most is the other's happiness. This kind of love isn't selfish, there's no expectation of return. You act for the other because the love in your heart is bubbling over. Get what I'm saying?"

"Sure." I understood perfectly because it was exactly how I felt about Dobie.

"I'll tell you something I've never told anyone—why I sometimes hate my job." She leaned closer and lowered her voice to confide in me about herself for the first time since I'd known her. "People come to me to talk about their relationships, but I know they're nowhere close to being capable of a mature relationship. Of course, I can't tell them that, so we beat around the bush and talk nonsense—he did this, she did that." She grabbed handfuls of her hair and pretended to pull it out. "You included! You've come for years with your relationship problems, but I knew you weren't ready for a truly mature relationship with a woman. So I've circled the periphery trying to get you to go inside, but I think you're damn close, and I'm happy for you."

# An Old Chicken Bone

When Dobie began losing weight, it didn't concern me. Some people get thin as they age, others get fat, and I supposed it was no different with dogs. Dobie was well past her thirteenth birthday, and since the life expectancy for Dobermans is ten to eleven and less for Rottweilers, we were in uncharted territory. But when she woke with the glands in her throat swollen to the size of oranges, her cheeks and jaws filled with fluid, and her sweet face resembling a grotesque chipmunk's, I took her back to the vet. Mark performed a biopsy of the lymph nodes. His manner was brusque and his eyes narrowed when he looked at me, but he said nothing.

A few days later, Mark called me to his office and handed me the lab report. It was positive for lymphosarcoma, an aggressive cancer. "It's advanced."

"What can we do?" I asked.

He handed me a vial of pills. "Give her these twice a day."

"What are they?"

"Steroids to reduce inflammation. It'll make the best of her last days. It's all I can do for her."

"Last days?" I was not quite allowing it to sink in.

Mark put his hand on my shoulder. "If she makes it past three weeks, I'd be very surprised."

Three weeks!

I administered the prescription for two days, but Dobie became overheated and panted incessantly. She seemed to lose her spirit on the drug, so I stopped it. To let her die with self-respect would be easier on both of us. But after discontinuing the steroids, she didn't improve. She lost her appetite and refused to drink.

On the positive side, her spirit seemed to perk up a little. The rattle of my car keys prompted her to rise to her feet and make an effort to accompany me on a walk. She still refused food and drink, but this time I watched her closely so she wouldn't become dehydrated. I kept her alive with electrolytes, powdered supplements, and yogurt and honey mixed with water. Three times a day, I squirted this liquid diet down her throat with a syringe.

After ten days, Dobie's strength was gone. Her legs, like rubber, could barely support her. She couldn't make it down the stairs on her own and had to be helped into the car. Once on her feet, she didn't have the power to climb the slightest incline. It didn't seem likely she'd last even the three weeks Mark had given her. She wasn't enjoying life, and I vowed that when the time came, I'd let her go. I made the appointment to put her to sleep.

It was Friday, and the mercy treatment was scheduled for Monday. It seemed a good idea to spend our last hours together in the country. Dobie would enjoy being amid nature, and it would be a way to say our goodbyes—goodbye to the places she loved and goodbye to each other. We went on one of our favorite walks, an easy two-mile hike with a gentle grade. Many times, I had to stop and wait for her. She could only travel one-fifth the speed of my normal walking gait.

Dobie still refused food and could manage only brief periods of exertion. We spent the majority of our time in the yurt. As we rested, I thought that visiting the country hadn't been a good plan. Dobie could barely walk, so obviously she didn't enjoy the hike. And now that the sun had set, the temperature dropped. I shook my head as I watched Dobie resting on the floor, a cold draft flowing steadily over her. She was a living skeleton, and the fasting had dangerously lowered her body temperature. Even covered with warm blankets, she shivered pitifully.

I had a long-standing rule of no animals on the bed under any circumstances, even a futon on the floor of a yurt, a resolution brought about by Big Pal's losing control of his bowels as he got old. But now I broke the rule and called her over. She didn't respond. She appeared to be deep in sleep, so deep I hastily checked for a heartbeat. As I lifted her onto my futon, I was surprised to feel how light she'd become. She was exhausted and didn't wake up as I nestled her onto the bed, her head flopping like a dead thing.

Her frailty was a knife in my heart. I wished the hands of time would fly faster. If only it were Monday so I could take her to the vet and end her misery. I chided myself for keeping her alive this long. I whispered into Dobie's ear that I wanted her to move on, I begged her to go. I wanted her to be free and happy, and I released her from whatever responsibility she felt toward me. Silently, I hoped her passing would go as peacefully as possible.

Monday morning we were back in the city. Dobie's appointment wasn't until three, and we went for a short walk in the park. Tears blurred my vision as I watched her totter jerkily on unsteady legs. Not long ago, her powerful muscles danced beneath a coat of black satin. She'd run like the wind and climb hills like a mountain goat. I was almost to the car when I looked back at Dobie trailing behind about five hundred feet. Her head was bent down, and she appeared to be sniffing something. I ran over to get a better look.

Was I hallucinating? After fasting for 13 days and refusing all the good food that had been offered, she was steadily munching on a rancid chicken bone! Dumbfounded, I went to the store and bought some chicken, and this time cooked it to make it warm and added a dash of soy sauce. She accepted a few pieces from my hand, and later in the day she ate more.

I happily canceled the appointment with Mark.

# A Tenth Life

Dobie went through more than the nine lives supposedly allotted to cats. The fasting had left her extraordinarily weak, but the lymph glands in her neck had shrunk, and her face lost its hideous swelling. It seemed as if she'd intuitively known how to care for herself during this last health crisis—better than me, or even the vet. To this end, she ate only tiny bits of food for an additional week and then began eating regularly. Soon she wolfed down two full meals a day of chicken, brown rice, and flaxseed oil. I was thrilled just to see her eat. Each meal gave her the strength to go on a little longer.

I thought she was as thin as nature would allow, yet the progression of the cancer and the fasting left her more emaciated than ever. She had no fat on her body, and even the large thigh muscles had wasted into meager strips of flesh. Her skin drew tightly over her bones, emphasizing every edge and contour of her skeletal structure. The unnatural way her ribs and bones poked out caused a reaction in those who saw her. Some would express compassion and concern, others became angry. "Some people shouldn't be allowed to own an animal if that's the way they care for it!"

The heart and courage Dobie displayed were extraordinary. She trudged up steep hills, which, at this point, must have seemed more like work than enjoyment but were necessary to keep the blood and lymph moving. I often turned back to see the spirit shining in her eyes as she gamely followed me up the hills, although I noted with sadness that the distance between us grew day by day. I'll forever be in awe of the powerful determination Dobie maintained to continue living in such a debilitated body. She simply refused to give in. There were days, even weeks, she didn't feel well. I, who knew her so intimately, could discern the times when she was down, in pain, or spaced out. Yet she kept on.

The days and weeks passed, and Dobie's strange recovery continued. Her presence was remarkably intense during this time, like the brightening flame of a dying candle. It was hard to believe she once evoked fear. Now she drew people like a magnet. Complete strangers went out of their way to approach and ask about her. Some put their arms around her and embraced her on the spot. One woman was so impressed that shortly after meeting Dobie, she went to the pound and adopted a Doberman puppy of her own. Perhaps television's fierce portrayal of Dobermans as guard dogs has given them a reputation as aggressive and mean. Unless one is familiar with the breed, it's hard to know how sweet a Doberman can be.

But despite my happiness that she seemed to be thriving, it was a tense, confusing time for me. Again I sought the counsel of Jen Clark.

We walked in, Dobie straining at the leash and sniffing Jen's office with excitement before settling down on the thick carpet. Generally preferring the rug to a chair anyway, I sat next to her. Jen shrugged, dropped down, and joined the crowd on the floor.

"For an animal on her last legs, the wonder dog looks fantastic. Did you have another shamanic dream?" She seemed half-serious, half-playful.

"No dreams. But it doesn't make sense to me either. Dobie has terminal cancer. Our vet gave her three weeks to live. It's now been twelve. I don't understand how she could live this long. Or why she seems so healthy."

Dobie was lying close to me, her body lightly touching my feet. With both of us looking at her, Dobie opened her eyes, lifted her head and pushed it against my hand so that I might pet her. She needed to be touched, to be loved, and she never stopped asking for it. As I rubbed her body, she sighed with contentment.

"She's quite the lover," Jen said. "Is she always like this?"

I nodded. "It's our evening activity. We sit together, her head in my lap, me massaging her. If I stop for even a moment, she'll push me with her head as if to wake up my hand. But you know, I never get tired of it."

"It's amazing the way that dog looks at you."

The love that shone in her eyes never diminished. If anything, it intensified as the strength of our bond grew.

"Don't you see?" Jen said.

"What?"

"You asked why she's still alive. That dog loves you too much to let go."

"Funny, I just met someone who said something similar."

"Is that right?"

"I was teaching a workshop in California a few weeks ago, and a woman I'd never met before came up to me and said, 'Your dog just spoke to me.'"

"Really?"

I laughed. "That's exactly what I said to her. She said she was an animal psychic."

"What exactly did she tell you?"

I rolled my eyes. "That Dobie is very unhappy because she doesn't want to leave me but knows there's just a little time left before she's got to go. She thinks Dobie's worried 'cause I won't have anyone to look after me the way she's done for all these years."

Jen cocked an eyebrow quizzically.

"I asked, 'Doesn't Dobie like my girlfriend?' She said, 'It's not that she has anything against her. She's just worried no one will be as constant as she's been.'"

Jen looked at me. "Doesn't sound too far off, but you obviously have a different opinion."

"If Dobie talks, why doesn't she speak to me?"

"Maybe she does."

"I don't hear anything."

"For a natural healer, you're kind of close-minded."

"I prefer practical and down-to-earth."

Jen rubbed her forehead. "You might get so close to earth that something bites you in the ass."

"At least I'll know it's real. I just don't like to talk about things I don't know. I can't say until I've had the experience."

Jen laughed. "Maybe you're right. Those who say they know don't, and those who talk the most know the least. So I guess I'd better shut up."

## Dobie's Rule of Love

Early November, a rare sunny stretch of weather, and Dobie feeling so well we went back to the yurt for another weekend in the country. We arrived late and, after a quick dinner, went straight to bed. It was just above freezing when the first light broke in a steel-gray sky. I fired up the Coleman camping stove and boiled some water for tea. It was our practice to get a little exercise after breakfast, and I called her for a walk, but Dobie was gone. I stood on the platform of the yurt, looking out into the forest. There she was, about three hundred yards away, nose in the dirt, scouting chipmunks. I put my hands to my mouth and yelled. She turned her head briefly and then returned to the hunt. No surprise. She wasn't smart in the classical sense of following orders to sit, stay, heel, or do tricks. Nor—like now—was she even obedient. She might listen if it went along with her plans, but if she'd rather be doing something else, she'd pretend not to hear.

A surprisingly strong sun was already breaking up the clouds as we went on our hike, the same one Dobie had such trouble with the last time we were here. This time she ran, chased chipmunks, and, besides being just plain old, looked fantastic. At the bridge, where we usually turned around, Dobie jumped into the ice-cold water and was so energized we continued up the road for miles, stopping only when the elevation rose high enough that we ran into snow. We must have walked 15 miles and didn't get back until late in the afternoon.

After a hearty dinner, we sat by the warmth of an open fire, listening to the sound of the flames licking the wood. An occasional pop sent a shower of sparks spiraling up on the air currents. There's something elemental about fire, especially on a dark, cold night. Staring into the flames was almost hypnotic. Thoughts unraveled. What would my life have been like if I hadn't met Tom on that foggy day in Stowe? It staggered my mind how we'd even found each other in that thick soup. But I no longer believed in accidents or random quirks of fate. When two beings are meant to be together, they inexplicably attract and connect. It was over fourteen years ago in Vermont when I'd first set eyes on Dobie. That sticky summer evening, Tom was acting strangely. He led me to the crowded, dirty cage where Dobie was living with the other puppies from the litter. At the time I was clueless, but destiny was being perfectly executed. Dobie and I were meant for each other.

I can still hear Tom saying, "Take her. You'll be saving her life."

It could be argued that I'd saved Dobie's life. I may have rescued her from a miserable existence, and, certainly, she saved my life more dramatically on that mountaintop.

The heat from the fire soon brought out the fatigue from the day's exertion. Dobie was asleep on a blanket and I was nodding off. I let her crawl into the sleeping bag with me. She lay with her head tucked against my side. I fell asleep quickly, but my eyes popped open after what seemed like a short while. It was still dark, and through the skylight of the yurt, there was only an ethereal glow from a slender moon. My watch said two o'clock. Everything was still and quiet. The normally soothing roar of the river seemed almost jarring, like the noise of a refrigerator when one has insomnia. The dark and the cold were restrictive; I couldn't do anything but lie there, thoughts assailing me, overwhelming thoughts I'd avoided for a long time. But in the almost absolute stillness of a northern rain forest, they beckoned, irrepressible. My chest and stomach felt tight and anxious. I knew it was coming, looming so close that it was hard to even enjoy these last moments. "There isn't much time before she must leave," the dog psychic had said. I'd scoffed and belittled it. But belittling is just a defense. Of course, she was right. And yet this weekend Dobie seemed so strong—as she'd always been. I'd never forget her determination as she fought through every obstacle in life, but it dawned on me for the first time that her strength was different from what I believed strength to be.

I believed myself strong and prided myself on it. But as I lay in the sleeping bag, I became more and more humbled by the falseness of my ways. Inside, I quivered like a leaf in a storm, clinging desperately to what was hidden. Lying in the darkness with Dobie by my side, it was clear that no amount of physical power could hide who I was, though I'd spent many years trying—covering the young, tender, unloved parts of myself that were so hungry yet too afraid even to ask for sustenance.

Strangely, within the tenderness, I glimpsed true strength beyond the strutting, boasting defensiveness I'd mastered. Dobie had put her head in my lap and begged for love. My straining muscles were exhausted. They could no longer hold back what was inside. Frozen tears fell as fresh blood softens an ancient scar. The empty place in my heart and the tightness in my gut were the places to explore. Perhaps, in these most tender places, I would find Dobie's secret.

But this, too, was a form of deception that wouldn't hold up to the cold scrutiny of the night. There was nothing to seek or find. I already knew her secret. I'd watched it begin as a mere trickle, and then, through life, sickness, pain, and inevitable death, it developed into a mighty river that flowed through her heart. She didn't own or hold it but let it pass through her to touch others. And as love flowed, it chipped away at the fear and healed her. She'd undergone the mysterious alchemy of the heart: the hard softened, melted, and—as the raging spring waters clear logjams—that which was stuck moved, untangled, and let go. And again she trusted in life.

It had taken her entire life—and her approaching death—for me to understand. I'd always wondered why fate had paired me with such a wounded animal. I believed, in my compassion and largeness of heart, that I'd healed her. But Dobie never stopped pouring into me and filling me with her love. Her heart was a literal lifeline, for with her love came a softening and brightness to my world. She opened me and showed how simple it can be. Without even knowing there was a lesson, she taught that the exchange of love is the true joy and purpose of living. Until this instant, I had not fathomed that, through it all, she was healing me.

# THE LAST HIKE OF THE SEASON

Dobie's spirit may have been willing, but her body had been ravaged by cancer, and her immune system taxed to the limit. It took all her energy just to stay alive. In such a weakened state, one becomes prey to secondary infections, and sure enough, Dobie developed a respiratory infection. She had a lot of phlegm in her lungs and hacked and gagged while trying to cough it up. Every time I touched her body, I could feel the progression of the disease. Previously, only the glands in her throat and chest were swollen, but now every lymph node in her body was rock-hard. Most inflamed of all were those in her throat, which made her life more difficult because there was less room for air in the passageway.

The first time Dobie retched and choked on her phlegm, I panicked and called Mark. When he picked up the phone, I blurted out what was going on. He was astonished that she was still alive; he'd assumed she'd passed months ago.

"There's not much anyone can do at this point," he said, "but I'd recommend putting her to sleep before she chokes to death."

Once again, I was faced with putting her to sleep. On one hand, I thought it best to let her go before she suffered further. Certainly, choking on her own phlegm wasn't the way. But she was still eating, drinking, and walking. She was trying so hard and, except for the gagging, had a decent quality of life. She was certainly still capable of loving.

I spoke with a friend.

"Dobie wants very much to be with you. Why take that away from her? She'll let you know when the time has come."

His words sounded right—probably because they were exactly what I wanted to hear. I started an aggressive treatment to shrink the glands in her throat. If I could reduce the inflammation, there'd be more room, and she'd have an easier time dealing with the phlegm. I gave her massive doses of germanium, garlic, antioxidants, and coenzyme Q10. After a few days, Dobie seemed to improve.

That weekend, Maria and I went to the coast. We hiked for five or six miles up a steep grade. Dobie greatly enjoyed it. She'd race up the hills and stand smiling, triumphant, seemingly free of pain, waiting for us to catch up with her. The power she still had in her body was amazing.

During the evening, however, the choking became worse. Again, I made the appointment to put her to sleep. I had steeled myself, but when face-to-face with Mark, I wavered. We sat for a long moment not saying anything. Mark looked at me, waiting for me to make the next move.

"We both know why I'm here," I finally said, "but what's your opinion?"

Mark didn't make it easy. He looked Dobie over and gave reasonable support for putting her to sleep but leaned toward treating her. He wanted to administer an antibiotic and continue with the anticancer therapy I'd started.

"I think you're on the right track," he said. "If the respiratory infection can be cleared, Dobie's incredible will to live just might be enough to pull off another miracle."

If there was even a shred of hope, I was willing to try. I gave Dobie the prescription, along with megadoses of supplements. But that very night, she took a turn for the worse. She was up for hours, choking and gasping for breath—slowly drowning in her own phlegm. At daybreak, we took our usual walk, but she was much more lethargic than ever before. In the morning she didn't touch her breakfast, and I could barely choke down mine. The food seemed to catch on something as it went down my throat. My body and heart knew what my mind was having so much trouble accepting: the end had come.

## The Circle Closes Sweetly

Dobie went upstairs to my office and waited for my first patient. When he arrived, Dobie greeted him and lay on the rug by the heater, resting peacefully. After a few minutes, she started to choke horribly. I couldn't take it anymore. Every time she retched, my heart jumped. I did something I'd never done before: sent the patient home without finishing, canceled the rest of the day's appointments, and rescheduled with Mark.

We had about an hour before it was time to leave. I took some pictures as a memento of her last day. I looked at her objectively through the lens of the camera. Dobie was painfully thin, her stomach bloated. She looked fatigued—as do all creatures when they don't feel well—yet the undying love and incredible spirit still shining in her eyes proved yet again that spirit and heart are masters of the flesh. After taking the pictures, I sat quietly, trying to appreciate our last minutes together. Dobie hoisted herself up from her bed and walked over to her untouched breakfast. She ate the entire meal and drank some water. And yet she looked so weary. There didn't seem to be any joy in taking nourishment. She acted as if it were a job that needed to be done even though the final sands were trickling through the hourglass.

As I watched her, I saw the folly in letting her go on. Left to her to make the decision, she'd never give up. She'd continue to hold dearly to life. She'd hold her spirit in a house with a leaky roof and collapsing walls until it was no longer possible to do so. It was up to me now to let go and let her move on.

With a traditional vet, the pet is ushered in and the lethal injection almost immediately administered. I've had animals put to sleep like this, and it's as shocking to the pet as it is to its guardian. I'd carefully watched Big Pal as he received the fatal shot. When the powerful drug was injected into his bloodstream, he was visibly jolted. It happened so quickly that his spirit must have been jerked from his body. It felt wrong, but Mark had a big heart and was way ahead of me.

"First, I'll sedate Dobie with Valium. As she relaxes, there'll be plenty of time for saying goodbye. By the time the farewells are complete, she'll be calm and feeling good. Only then will I administer the final injection."

I liked his philosophy. There'd be no terror or fear. She wouldn't even see it coming.

Mark shaved a patch of hair off Dobie's arm and then gave her the injection of Valium. Dobie took a few steps and immediately became rubber-legged. She couldn't stand on her feet. Quickly, I got down on the floor, leaned her body against mine, and placed her head on my lap. Within seconds her eyes rolled back in her head. She was completely unconscious.

"I'm surprised the Valium affected her so strongly," Mark said. "They usually just get really relaxed."

It showed how little energy she had left, how frail she actually was.

Dobie was completely out before the lethal injection came anywhere near her. She must have felt only sweetness as the cord was severed and her spirit soared freely, released, at last, from the fetters of her diseased body.

I thought I was prepared for this moment. Dobie and I had been through our brushes with death before. But whatever preparation I thought I had was bogus. I didn't want Mark or his staff to see me cry, and I called on every ounce of self-control to make an attempt at composure. But as if by a will of its own, my face contorted and the silent tears fell freely.

Mark put a hand on my shoulder. "Do you want me to take care of the body?" We'd previously discussed his cremation service.

"No, thanks," I quavered.

I picked her up and, with my friend's still warm, limp body in my arms, stumbled out of Mark's office.

# Happy Hunting Grounds

Portland has an ordinance against burying pets within the city limits, but it wasn't the law that stopped me. I didn't want to bury Dobie in the city; I preferred to lay her body on our land in the country, where she'd spent her happiest days. Of course, the part I'd loved had already left, and from that perspective, it mattered very little what was done with the physical body. Still, I wanted to honor my friend as much as possible.

On the way out to the country, there were several stops to be made. One was the grocery store. Maria, who'd come along to support me, hadn't eaten. I insisted she have a little something, and we pulled into the parking lot of a Safeway to pick up a couple of yogurts. Before getting out of the car, I covered Dobie's body with a blanket so only her head peeked out; I didn't want to startle anyone who might see her lying in the backseat. Just as we were returning to the car, a woman pulled into the spot next to us. She got out of her vehicle, glanced into my backseat, and, to my surprise, flashed me an isn't-that-precious smile.

When we arrived in Rhododendron, I inspected the burial site I'd started months ago when I thought Dobie couldn't possibly make it much longer. The hole needed finishing work, but the task was difficult because the ground was hard with frost. While trying to chip away at the frozen earth with a shovel, I was tempted to give up and settle for a shallow grave. But how could I? Dobie never, ever gave up. The job had to be done right. I lined the hole with a sheet and covered Dobie's body with a tapestry from Thailand. As I bent down to hug the body that only hours ago had housed the spirit I loved so much, I drew in a quick breath. Five or six hours had elapsed since the euthanasia, yet her open eyes hadn't clouded over. There was no sign of decay or rigor mortis. I've heard yogis say it's the mark of a saint if, after death, the physical body doesn't decay. Dobie didn't look dead at all. Her face was as peaceful and beautiful in death as it had been in life. Now I understood why the woman in the parking lot had given such a smile.

It was good that the weather was clear and the moonlight allowed me to stay longer. I filled her grave with dirt and erected a rock sculpture from the stones I'd unearthed while digging the hole. Maria lighted seven candles and we burned some incense. I started to mumble a few words about her life, but words seemed lame and inadequate; they grated against the quiet of the country twilight. Maria and I stood silent in the descending night. As the stars thickened, glinting like powdered diamonds on a velvety winter sky, I recalled an Eskimo proverb: Perhaps they are not the stars, but rather openings in heaven where the love of our lost ones shines down to let us know they are with us.

Dobie's grave, with its rock-sculpture marker and flickering blue candles, spread a peaceful feeling into the forest. The wind rushed through the tall firs, and the bubbling river provided eternal music. I was satisfied with the ceremony and pleased that Dobie's body was resting close to the yurt, in the heart of chipmunk-hunting grounds— the very place she'd spent so many happy hours.

## Reunion in Dream Time

Soon after Dobie's death, I had a dream. I drove up to a small comfortable-looking cabin, pulled into the driveway, and opened the door. Dobie was lying on the couch. We played the same game we had when she was alive: when she saw me, she quickly jumped off—she knew she shouldn't be up there, but we both knew she practically lived there—and ran over to greet me. She wasn't emaciated anymore but full, sleek, and as healthy as she'd been in her prime. She got up on her hind legs and I came down on my knees. We were face-to-face and put our arms around each other. Somehow she was able to do that.

The following night, again, I visited the cabin. Dobie greeted me, and we went outside and walked down a path alongside a gigantic river with a raging current and huge waves that ebbed and flowed. Soon we entered a wilderness more wild and expansive than anything I'd ever seen.

And for a third night, I dreamed. This time we stayed in the house. Dobie curled up next to me on the rug. I held her head in my hands and stroked her while she loved me with her eyes. Even in the dream I was struck by how much love flowed through her dark eyes and entered my heart.

I had a session with Jen Clark.

"I wanted to ask you about some dreams I've been having."

"More dreams." Jen smiled. "How's Maria?"

"She broke up with me and left for Idaho."

Jen looked surprised. "Two big losses in a row. How're you holding up?"

"I miss Dobie, but there's no regrets. A long time ago, when she was a puppy, I vowed I'd take care of her for the full cycle of her life, and I did."

"It was touching, the way you cared for her."

"She gave me a lot more."

Jen cocked an eyebrow. "Your dreams?"

I told Jen about them. "You know, it's not much different than when she was alive."

"Do you believe in your dreams?"

I paused for a few seconds. "I don't necessarily believe Dobie's living in a house by herself in another dimension, or that she still looks like she did when she was alive. Maybe I see her dog body just because it's familiar to me. But I do believe we're connecting somehow, because our hearts want to—like that Gibran story. I'll never know for sure, but that's okay. Some things are better kept as a mystery."

Jen laughed. "My reluctant shaman, always the skeptic. So why did Maria leave?"

"She wasn't ready for a serious relationship and needed some space to find herself."

"How do you feel about that?"

"I've no problem with her. Maybe Maria was an angel who

came to support me through the roughest times with Dobie."

"Now you're talking, and don't worry, my friend. There'll be more Marias." Jen gazed at me evenly. "Lots of them, if you want."

After a long silence, I said, "I finally understand why I kept meeting him on the road."

"Meeting who?"

"My old neighbor, the recluse. You once asked why I kept meeting him."

"Okay, why?"

"We were the same, he and I. Had the wind blown a few degrees differently, I could have been him."

"But you took a different path."

"I had a good teacher."

# Epilogue

Animals, it is sometimes said, are no more than beasts operating with instinctual drives originating from a primitive mammalian brain. But I like to think that animals, like humans, move with their own destinies. Dogs, as silent messengers, call to those whose hearts are lacking that most essential ingredient for survival. Perhaps, as was the case with me, one may not know how much they're in need; yet the canine healer appears not when we expect it but when, on the inside, a corner has been turned and we're ready to open. Their love doesn't judge, keep score, or threaten. It's a safe, unassuming love that sneaks up to soothe what has been broken and open that which is closed. We may never comprehend how they move with the mystery as healers, protectors, and bringers of light. Or how, when they leave the earth's dusty trails, their task has been so well-accomplished. Their love doesn't perish but grows and spreads, passing ever onward on the endless web of life.

The sentinel that marks Dobie's life is a simple cairn of gray stones, stacked on top of each other and held only by gravity.

I believe she'd prefer it this way. When I'm no longer here to rearrange what winter storms dislodge, all that will remain is the forest's green ground cover, the white and purple trilliums that of late have grown where she lies, and the silent rocks. They won't tell whose bones rest here, or how she lived her life. So after the snows melt, I replace the fallen stones.

And I may linger by her grave awhile, pondering the trails we walked and the mystery that brought us together.

We would appreciate it if you would review our book online.
Thank you!

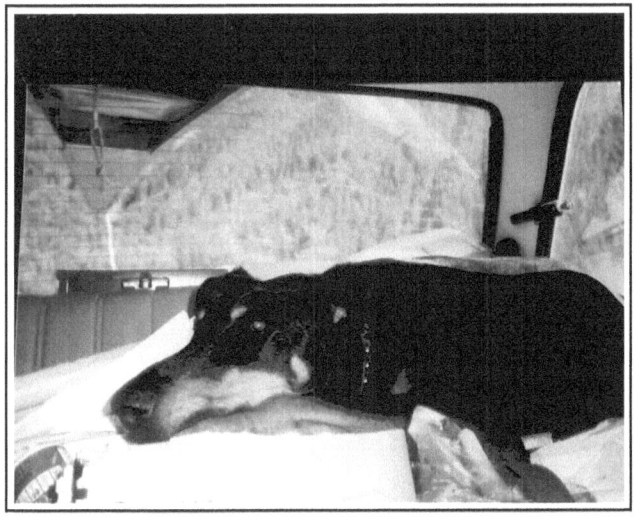

*10% of the profits from*
***Dobie, The Canine Saint***
*will be donated to Animal Aid*
*animalaidpdx.org*

Soon To Be Released by Paul Greenbaum:

## The Cage Fighter

*Before he can face the MMA champion, Johnny will have to face himself.*

"Everyone's got the flaws, but few have what it takes to look at them."

Johnny Lazio's life as an undefeated MMA fighter crashes into the vicious fist of Antonio Morales, who breaks not only Johnny's nose, but also his confidence. As he flounders, his coach frets that Johnny might never be able to bounce back. His karate Sensei turns away in shame.

There's only one person who can reach Johnny in his low point—a young Thai prostitute named Cindy, who draws Johnny out of his almost monastic life and starts to lead him back inside himself.

# About the Author

Paul Greenbaum is a chiropractor acupuncturist in practice for over 20 years. He loves to write more than almost anything.
If you are interested in more of Paul's work see:

**drpaulgreenbaum.com**
or
**takeyourhealthinyourownhands.com**.

www.ingramcontent.com/pod-product-compliance
Lightning Source LLC
Chambersburg PA
CBHW030445300426
44112CB00009B/1169